Out of Nothing

QR Hand is everything in *Out of Nothing*. He is omnipresent, a philosopher, a voice from the edge, a last dance to a classic song playing in the mind of a quintessential poet. This essential work is bare of filigree and void of pretense, it is a reasoned accounting of a well-known world, earmarked and noted in all the margins by an astute tactician. This work dances deftly on the edges of razors cutting deep and clean.

– Ayodele Nzinga, author of *Sorrowland Oracle*

QR Hand was a lot of things and his poems are a lot of things. I watched him call lightning on a stage, in a dining room, in a car on the way to a reading. I watched him sing things apart and sing them healed. I heard him roll out 1960s advertising jingles, Dodgers lineups, and poems that shook the hinges of the doors of greed and privilege. I knew him silly and wise and troubled. There are few truths that can't be learned from his poems. Carry them with you.

– Kim Shuck, author of *Exile Heart*, 7th Poet Laureate of San Francisco Emerita

QR Hand is the quintessential jazz poet as he bends, stretches, conflagrates and dissects passions and ideals and the tragedies of our times taking a humming electron microscope to the details of living, of war mongering, of street hustling and of surviving across cultural landscapes and geographic chasms. Then with a change in tempo he creates a telescope showing us how many galaxies we live inside and give birth to. qr hand shapes his poems in the way a jazz master does, curving notes and stretching keys and playing universes inside the chord changes of a familiar song which bring you to places you never knew existed.

– devorah major, author of *califia's daughter*, san Francisco's 3rd Poet Laureate

Out of Nothing

QR Hand Jr.

BLACK FREIGHTER PRESS

CONTENTS

Gotcha

in the forest
on the hills
overlooking the sea and the ocean
on the green island
under the less than half moon
he lights the candle
breathes deeply
begins to play his drum
to the night

in east harlem
overlooking the new york new haven and hartford trucks
elevated above park avenue
he is lighting his candle
looking at his drum

on the lower east side
by candle light
he is playing his drum
concentrated sweating
carib thought rhythms

he has stopped drumming
the sun begins its squint across the horizon
in accra he is getting ready
to blow out his candle
and walk in his day

in the forest
on the hills
overlooking the sea and the ocean
on the green island

you look to cuba and africa from
on the right spot
in the hills the marines do not know
the island they take water from
to feed the growing refinery
on saint croix
he knows san juan is dark

puerto rico was dark last night
the lights are out in puerto rico

who's got the power
who's got the power
who's got the power

who's got the power

Looking Back At You

Cooptation call it   shared   how cultures work on   and
in the courts   where   the quick tongued move dollars   and
Lives from one side to an other   most valuable killers
Running rampant like panzers   and   shermans   and
Goulds   and   Rhodes   in the heart   or   trained in the
Oran genocide in the hands   on the way to find

the gold   and   other appropriations in the name of
I'm gonna kill if you don't do what I say   and   might
Even if you do it

All that's why lotsa people(s) are all ways makin' lotsa
Revolution(s)

Comments on causa humana   there   affirming their ways
And   the right to appropriate   or   not   as well as being appropriated
Trying to be appropriate in the ways of nature   may be not
As constant as several millennia ago but plugged in
Never the more   or   less   mobiles   mermaids on their hoods
Hooting too late for desotos   la salles   and   coronados busting out
In these new free doms   and   tents of their own choice

Undigested pap swillers on the fence of the markets
Raising the young for war   whose   the killers   whose   the
Victims played in all those towns   and   places close
To city out skirts   where   told mighty music came rolling from
There   the final   tiffanator's drummer   the one with all those

Automatic (weapons or whats)
Lotsa nuthin' stacked   a sta5h of south American powders
Here   and   there be tween volumes of hard written notes of
World wide cops inc

Killers   shark repellent never worked in the first place no matter
How much distributed in search of killing rules   please
Of the wake   pleas of the wake   the ugh no's afraid to walk
Through those gates   doors to an abrupt in stops
Rolling heads on the side walks   one of which is yours

Looking back at you laughing maniacally   multiplying
And   you escape to the lions'den   praying for their mercies
Giant feline noblesse oblige   a member of some kinda packs
Like your selves xpecting a miracle   bugle   and   cavalry
when a drone won't work any more   union or not
The media may be too late to catch your demise   like che
To read the unreadables   all the unreadables on time's desk top !!

The Speed of the Times

Up dating alice's wonder land   bleeding hearts   and
Lines of credits flooding drenched plains
Generations stoopified   bent in famines

What's a place like this supposed to be like any how
How any   how many a trumpet note grabs mind
In its wander   no wonder to this

You can listen to musics concertedly
Hoping the song is there   a swing freeer   and   a sling gunner
All of this while the boss is on a vacation   yatching
Around a changing world   a whirl   a whirl wind   a plenty

more immediate persons in my dreams   even
The dead (ones)   still   just goin' back   and   forth   in the swing
Of things   and   their orbits   and   momenta   ta ta

The chickens are dying   and   I'm not   so far
When it was bennies   the speed of the times   all
The druggists in harlem   the black ones any how   knew
What that drummer Blakey comin' 'round   lookin' in
When you hit it   smokin'   but   right at some body   and   thinkin'
About a game of inches   for your mama   the bright
Side of things   bright   and   shining   lies   neil
Wrote about   and   some   we knew were off the chart
Smarter than the law allowed   yet   out laws of course

Reluctantly accepting the change in season   as
October is the day after tomorrow   and   a breeze
To come with it   harvest moon gone   garden turning
Dried out   crispy like   waiting for the rainy season   we think
Is coming this year of no Indian summer at all

Hate winter's coming on   knowing thank fully it ain't like
The apple   or   the 'cuse   or   philly too   as I realize
Snow   and   storm go from fun   to   hassle   to   persecution
By natural forces making poems from lines blown about
The hood hiding from the hawk in door

Ways   and   tunnels through the archeologies about to be
Launched under the hinter lands   cables
Fine   or   thick with fibrous tentacles sliding in
To plug in devices   and   phone attacks   ring-a-bling
Ding   ding   dong   and   don't ask whose number is

Being hacked   a future   or   dead ending spaced
Out of a loop waiting for the real deal at the foot
Of a cantankerous hill some Sisyphus gotta push you
Up   and   down   and   of course all around town   they
Knew what time you'd roll back hopin' to retrieve

Some of the box lunch they made for you for the trip
Up   and   of course they can't blame you for tryin'
Again tho' some think you need a better pusher
Man   or   woman   no room for sexism in serious
Matters

Threatening skys   to whom   just 'cause it's chilly   and   grey
All of 'em as good as new   like in a new porn shop
All buy his tone   some ness   who missed their x's   and   o's
So gates is that open   and   a kick offensives again
Where's the news here

If it just could have stayed the way we dreamed it even for
    a little while

what a par theid den chilluns
'trane blowin'   'trane blowin'
lee boppin' sweedom   'swe dom

Albizu singin' stars out
in to tropical nights'
sea blue green hills
glazing

che moon beaming love song
to sister breeze time

you
woman pearl dancer
shimmy me scarlet tranced
sun silver and purple
rayed in golden
swirl it in the palm wine
at dusk

skirt ballooning azalea upwards
loud flower macaw
to the beat
of all of the drums

flute crying sweetly on the beach
the mountains too are ours

Liberty or Death

And   she didn't have no body to be personal with   all   brown stones
Gone   and   gangs of dogs if you're lucky   '
Ruined country   sides right up to the stone world
Games on this corner   or   that one   and   you carry your own
Lights 'cause no public lights work   and   if you   and   your
People sing under the lamp post   but   don't wanna be targeted

By friend   or   foe   'cause it all most doesn't make any difference in
Some of these wards now   friends   and   enemies prayed
To the same gods   and   the active life of priests   ministers
Monks   nuns   prophets   saint   rabbi   any high mucketty
Mucks was short   couldn't be insured   some starved well

If stones were speaking to you as they danced to
One of the many musics unheard to your ears   but
Going on   and   on so many places
so much of earth   you're not part of   yet

Liberty   or   death to every version of your selves found   tho'
Deplored by the killing machines   no matter the version
And   the rationales in little white boots in slow advance
In their file of march safely with traveling bars
And   bordello   where   new acts highly guaranteed

A new child hood became the universal cry   its ugly
In here   and   wants out soon as possible   high ways of
Infinitude   plums   and   stones   out of the way place(s)
Scoring drought   oh didn't it rain   chasin' mamas off
Every corner   you raw   wet   catastrophes real   and
Imagined in door ways to locked stores empty of
Merchandise   and   then the portals to the front next door

There were blurps   and   bursts   and   belching weapons
Of gasses where all believed they were dead   and
Didn't have to participate any more   and   could return
To some thing they couldn't remember   but   chances are
No longer exist from the bottom of a 21st street   and   worse

Tryin' to look good was no good   and   what else was there
To do out of the window   off the roof   o.d. of the day
It was a man thing   and   of course you could do the war
Thing   jump outta planes   and   kill people after you land
If you weren't killed on the way down   it was duck soup   you

Know what you mean man kinda thing   string ears together
With your hands beats bein' a wino in an alley offa
Cat fish row   or   river side drive   don' forget route
66   manifest destiny in the raw   saddle up jack
And   jill show you looks that kill   thrill   or   mistake

And   hope you don't get caught   or   have to do time
On my head   and   hands   what a fuckin' vision
Or   view a swell foop in the lead   with a smile
Of all mighties' eyes   and   teeth all the way in place
Some how lucky through constant   continuous mayhem   or

Just plain rotten luck   deluge(s) of sheet(s) meant for
The front   but   you're here horrifically in the back yard
Waiting for the wild dogs to come   the greatest ire(s)
Are no right to great inhumanity   globe trotters being scored on
Incessantly   what strange creature this is here   left

Flowers Too Rare

If it wasn't for the fact that all those dreams were realer
Than shit   colored   blind   a whole race of offensive
Tackles   then   guards around tight ends tripping on
Bottles of rums left by retreating quarter tones owned by
A paper out fit in the caymans trying to take losses of others

Not too seriously 'cause the cayman navy is very small
And   even more non violent carrying a starter's pistol only
For barracuda races on track   and   on board only the best
Of rums   and   coke spoons passed about by drones
free to show thigh the whole time

Lots of ceremonial candles   flowers too rare now   but
Lots of pictures from way back whens   and   many of their ministers
And   now down to only their model t's as the clock keeps running
alarms as dead as door nails
Locked in by a crush of seconds   and   a slow sound system

humming birds' sweet fluxing   suspending this group   in
Dirt kicked up   it's a big why   on the horizon   falling

There   and   so many other places   you just had to be in a play
And   you were a wise clown   full of slow notions
Autre fois   my baby   autre fois   from the big boom box
Remembering   you weren't human really back then   and
It took years to find out   oh so too late now   what the hell

It don't mean a thing   but   so much is still   chasing you
Grimes of the centuries   no deterrents   detergents came
Later   no deterrents yet gravity risin'   dis   ordering every
Pattern   strategies   and   tactics   demanded much melting
Continued for a long time   that's the tale of its wandering   y   mas

before the fragmenting
Kablooie   and   a room full of tricks   kinda room the size of central
Park   if you knew new York

You remember to duck   and   if not   you'll never remember at any all
At all   time to find apetites before dying   they wanna
Clock 'em   you wanna glock 'em   make a hole of your enemy
Children of the universe   all ways targets   baby turtles slowly
Under a barrage of gulls   you know it's all gone   not a

Drop to kick you people(s)   where it hurt(s)   real bad
For a long time in side   excruciating   (s)   bolts   and   butter
Flying stabbings   exquisite this entry of what you want   your
Extremes   feeling(s) before surrender   and   cry for nurses of
Mercy   angels   or   not   but   you ain't got none   'a this fantasy

To save your ass from this suffering   or   think about morphine
As the good tool it is   'sposed to slow you down   but   you see
The hands   and   fingers of these musicians on sax   or   flute
Or   piano key after perfectly sequenced notes climbin' a ladder
That past you were never a part of   wasn't there

And   the lord   or   some mutha fuckas told old Orpheus
To sing his ass off   and   he had him a chorus of as many
Ghosts as real live mutha fuckas blasting the way in to an other
Place where every thing that could did the dance it could
With what evah creatures there was   and   them rocks stand

Risin   and   formin' a shing a ling line like they know this
Knowledge too   and   all this too was happening in the phenomenal
World where death had been exceeding its limits for a generation
Now   and   soon there may not be ruins to fight over

Blues Poem

black
black
black
blacker than black
blacker than black black black
blacker than that black
blacker than that black blacker

that black blacker than that
that black blacker than even that black
that black that blackens black blacker

blacker
blacker
blacker
blacker than that

and what black be blacker than that black

a black that blackens hallways in the south park
a black that blackens hallways in south bronx

or south american brazil nut black
or keys at the end of gyrating fingers rippling black ragtime
or joe black
or old black art from the sahara
or old black art from birdland
or black eldorados in mystery movie black

or brightly hiding sweet
at the end of the rainbow
black honey

As The Blood Grew

And   wives too   it's said   after black Friday panties frayed
Some place else passion   or   the pits   and   pith of a
Junior high script about why we get layed so late
In the day   won't let us out at nite   talkin' about all
The ustah be's   and   where   then   and   the sweetest

Music they said   and   of course   they were the last
Generation every body had to wear helmets   and
Carry gas masks   and   a package of pills   the last of
Which was called quick death   when the pain killers
And   last deep dream machines don't do nuthin'

No more   how many turn overs can you make before
They wheel in the guillotine   which by now was duller
And   slower   but   a new blade was an unnecessary expense
After a while   the public spectacle   where the player
Gets a chance to smoke   drink   drop   shoot up   or   main line

What ever combination   or   all   and   due to book keepers
And   street corner wisdom   lately   a player would look
Up   so he could raise his neck quickly   at the
Descending blade   other wise   it could be dread
Full   even for by standers   and   those on duty

Explaining this to visitors from other nations   who
Wanted to see the real old basket ballers being
Phased out ingeniously   and   even in war times
When deodorants weren't made any more the
Visitors claimed they could smell significant differences

Low   and   ardor   and   all the stars left after most left
After most never passed the patriotic profile test

After the buzzer went off   and   their things were confiscated
And   distributed among greedy on lookers   some of
Whom were genuinely hungry   others followed loot

An other big one   clown   giant   debt makin'   blood suckin'
twerps
They were   uniformly looking silly   and   giving orders   as if
They all ready owned   what they were taking   quite violently
Cold as hell   and   space heaters gone to the moon   but
Whose   they kept asking on the way to the tar pits

It's cold as hell   but   too late   as the blood grew
Thicker   and   slower   and   stories racing through the stars
And   constellations pasted in bed time stories   'cause
They keep saying   buy one   and   get one free   and   you got
A lot   all ready selling xmas trees for next year   your job

Singing   I didn't know what time it was   over   and   over
Pontifications over the river   and   through the woods
To grand mother's house we go   then   the grippe gotcha
And   then   there's the spy vs spy   at the same time   with
Its own body count   and   if this news ain't blues enough

Remember spys get more bucks than workers who gotta
Grub it   second hand minds   on the make   with wild west
Handlers   ready to chop off thumbs for suspicious trans
Actions   she was so many accidents you wanted to make
Sure didn't happen   and   whether the queen of sheeba

Helen of troy   or   foxey brown   lots were ready to lose
Small fortunes to stay in the chase   and   not be washed
A way in a wake of casualties   and   hearts   and souls
Lining imaginary high ways   of   lost loves   the sounds
Of many knives being sharpened   and   looking for meat(s)

Fox holes too deep to get out of   and   where do you
Shit at this end of the firing range   and   your
Pay goes down when you get hit   to stop the pain
You cut off life   as the leader who bought you here is
Re elected from his jail cell   but   can't pardon him self !!

Test

The sun is the only thing warm
As hearts are in freezers to keep
Well   not enough for a real
 Smorgasborg any more   limbs
And   eyes only now   and   they
Throw a way any thing over 7
As stiff with age   trying to invent
Televisions with out commercials
Buying time   stealing from laundromat

Washers   and   dryers   paying off tiny
Look outs with collected roaches skimmed
From neighbor hood vipers   and   their
Often visitors pointed out by the tiny ones
As if that's what they were born for   like
Chimney sweeps in a dingey dicken's tale
So terrible competing against brothers   and

Sisters to stay small   and   not be eaten
Having fewer birth days   putting candle makers
In to a precarity zone   and   the few basket ballers remaining
Had to accept small pensions   or   smaller cells
In the older walls be tween the reservations   so
Ecologically sound

And   financially responsible   where the will
To power's in a world of trouble   some   or all
Or   in the hall ways of that large apartment
At 112th street   and   7th avenue   across the street
From a little hotel   mortal   metal   medals   for
Valorous behaviors in the service of cosmetic prosthetics
For

Returnees of foreign wars who could no longer be
Hidden in zoos   and   circuses for the criminally insane
From the previous wars of valor   mortal metal   and
Honors for academics too old   or   sub versives   whose
Protesting often led to blood curdleing screams   in future

Protests in the court of too late for you   and   yours
If you got any yours left   and   then there's this
Dreary expiation   ain't the California I moved to
So much more blood flooding the plain than raining
Which gotta be pumped back   and   forth   and
In   and   out fuckin' travesty of water ways

Weighs a lot on all those draft dodgin' farmers
Lazy on the land   the very frumiousness of it
No longer just banter snatched in to a vortex   of
Meanings colliding on receding ideological tramps   and
Their directress   and   that distress at the redressology
Of it insufficient heft

They all said your draw bridge is down for
The clowns   and   farmers to cry in the streets
Teeming now flesh flood didn't come to California for
The rain   but   it's said this very earth needs it   if
They're gonna continue to make wars here   killing
As many possums as possible

Real   or   just playin' possum's a good enough kill
In some counties   (lithe mettle there now   bright
Sun up morning beams   bright poems wending centuries a
Way lika a saxophone solo in sweet jungle time(s)   and
Covering the tons of tripe they try to stuff drummers

With   speaking dreams   and   a fuller tongue   with
No words   and   vital sounds past   and   (i)   all ways
Wanted to stay on the earth   feet there   and   finding
Spirit in soil   eschewing the high in a sky I knew not   and
not to care for   but   in

A loving family   existing in such tensions   impacted beyond
Words it had stopped working   like constipations do a strike
In the harbor   hopes in be low deck   and   sit there
An operation going In after it   wearing so many hats
Determined   to my shit   your life   they say loud

First little break comes   then hoping   making the profound
Simple   yet heady   ducats for buckets   takin' it to the streets
All over the world   falling down   progressions   posters' high brio
And   lots of bottles   bruja   and   hubbub   a pun fight   at
An o.g. joint   hidden from draft boards

And Some Gentle

Terrible arms   and   their threatened uses
Give it up or we bomb your asses into parts
Of the rubble red crosses can't do nuthin' for

Comin'   and   goin'   the gahlute(s)   as victors   demand
With special word(s) their favorite meal
reserved now only for those in the capitol

written on those winds of their thoughts
the daily wisdom radio   which
spoke sporadically yet right too

citizens quizzed randomly on its content
And   meaning   and   failing   can mean loss of citizen ship

meaning teach or be disappeared

Any time you opened a jar   or   carton   or   box   or   bottle
Or the door of family cars
Reminding you how people greet each other

Or   hold 'em high jack   at the cross roads   and   some gentle
Too   land of loss all around me   so what   I'm still found
And   not alone

gonna give 'em a tale back   and then some   a
Novella   and   a romance in san juan   yaknow what I mean
Scrap(e)s from no thing(s) you wouldn't   but   it's so easy

Mind   a fog of absence(s)   and   there was madness in a
Throat of that creeping flock   sneakers on their wits
And   a hope to die   rollicking   what the fuck ability to high

Jump any time of night   in a corner of mirage   stitched in
To a collegial palette of mollusks   and   velvet   marbled

Murder by real estate   make poetry great again o' ye
Ravers   in edges   in the cities   20th century vipers
Flyin'   and   skyin'   revenge of the innocence   this paradise
walking algorithms nastier than seals   combat

Hidden on an us   and   a them   gone to the cleaners
It's a broth hiding in the scent of burning fur bottled
By the couth cauldron group   and   advisors of the coupon

Clipping class   snaggled truly   gleaning gleamers dreaming
Nightly   screaming weavers   the o.g. streakers   steaming
Towards higher horizons for better pill boxers   and   lines of new
Demarcations to slurp from in the bath of the front
Liners   and   clash timers   metrically bound   frightened speed

Demons   and   freaks   prattlers cemented to permanent wavers
On remaining shored up beach front properties   schemers
The bleaker than thous   welcome to paradise   no trespassing
Glory dead nation(s)   reparations   and   returning lands for a right
to kill

In This Universe

all hell's gonna bust loose lookin'
for the prayer

Hero one day   bum the next   like   traitor to patriot   and back
In this fish aspirating   the whale of a time it was   an

example   of a delicate brute

god knows   or   the goddess do   waiting for
The monsters in blue   they don't even know who marcus
Haines is   or   was   like goose tatum   and   sweet water Clifton

It didn't start with bobby Dylan   but   what if it did
Oh sun   oh sun   oh sun   oh sun   o'   do not desert us   do not
Do hot sun   do not desert us in the course of your
Business in this universe   ours   for an instance   of
Time   space   instantly gone

Made more wine   and   drank away the memories
Of the good times they kept making up   and   down

soul swindlers on the loose   ya know
Wadd I'm sayin he wuz sayin for every body to know
The pith of these thoughts laid out on the cutting board
And   too many razor backs in the runnin for killer of the year

the agents of the agencies
All those letters with periods   and   auto matic
Weapons after each   and   those agents had hearts
And   kiddies in the homes who wanted rides   and   drugs

None of the contracts   or   armed robberies mattered

Half the family was in on the take/fake   and   loyalty
Was a choice   or   a short very unhappy life had
Been known to happen   so   they got a new car

Whether things like this were happening(s) all over
Like history books were bound to say is true
'cause there was enough truth to leave in a structure
Down causing a real drop in values   so   when
The lights went out   and militias fired on each other

coffin makers richer in the name of the flag

Nameless

Who knows they said/say you says
But tell 'em or not it's a mystery

'cause every body know the kind
Of liar you are any how so they

They knows/know with out sittin'
Next to you there 'cause it was a kick
In the ass for who can't afford a chair
'cause they spends/spent it on a used
Kalesnikov spiffing it up and learning to
Clean it and take it a part and put it
Together   his wife and child
In his heart   talking of targets

            gold counts more than the other colors combined

The religions which create gross perversions
In the ledgers   of the laws   in the act of
Worshipping gods
There are mouths to feed   and   bills to pay

And   they say this is heaven   and
Don't look down 'cause some body
Could grabs/grab your ankle   and
You go flyin'
Ya know ending this episode

And   some time/times the machines break
Down like you do   and
That's the time to get 'em   with their pants
Down   trippin' over the selves now

31

Holy moley   and   hail mary   both   on the field(s)
With open goals   dump pimple/pimp   ample ass
Muthafuckas   and   their mamas   said the name
Of this game is 7 card stud   and   when's the best
Time for which pitchers really depends   the number(s)
Of rockets your constituents keep at home

In the basement freezer(s) under the steaks/stakes
Chops lamb   and   pork some got dope   and   bodies
There too   so what's a knuckle ball for the prowess
no matter giving up so no matter how often
They bury you   you get back up   and   invade again
A strike out you wanted to park that ball   but
So much dust   and   dope

      Peace keepers   blind to gore
      Here that ain't a broad side   a blitz kreig
      A murderers' row   a missed ball screeching
      To the oblivia

You stands   and   you shakes   and   breathe   and
Then   dance   if there's still a floor   and   look for
A drink blithely hoping people in the street got some
Thing good to smoke in the debris

Spladoosh

all aimed and not aimed at people make for interesting
    insurance policies

Made out to charities for so many   why not so long   and   a dios
    and   so long jack

electric costumes killing admirers so slow

Compare to round ball on the block   or   squatters' rights
In the frying pan of designers' visions   and   over there   some
One was selling futures   and   imaginations free of
Charges filed by the mothers y madres of
The play ground et al. against an Artaud
On the edge of this ghetto   and   this was just

An other rampant incredulity in halls   and
Back alleys of in justice with armies you
Don't got   and   think of all the hullabaloo
Gets lost in that piece of the canvas   too
raunchee to play at parties   but   after hours

in the dark   she sang it   again and again

a brand of on the corner doo whopping

before there was a thing to be named   music preceded

salsa on the menus of many in dance halls   and   bars   and   cafes
ustah you could have a good time out there   but   so much anger
and   guns is passed   knives   and   bottles   even an ax   or   2
so you stay at home   and   remember   or   talk to those who didn't
all about every detail   you never even know you knew   or   may

be not at all   but   the anthropologists might not know that
or   in these news times   everyone from down the block knows not
to snitch by tellin' as close to the truth as possible
and   some discretions are based on a class war
they have no experience in finding out tito preceded

let's dance the salsa in new York   or   san juan   or   Havana
and   there was real shit   before   they started selling you
bull shit in colors of real   but   some had the ears
that see   and   what about political realities so hard
to see in culverts of comforts   and   softening camemberts

from so many fine farms in this part of the
country   green   and   ripening
predictably   the part you'd hate to have a war in   but   the
colonels don't see it   and   you never plan for shell holes in
the fields   the lawn   the gardens   animals in psychoses
dithering idiots with frightened attentive children   posters in Arabic

all of this makes for a slowing down from certain angles   endorphins
their triviatatta   the crown of many things   so hear   being
pushed by captive full backs belching   and   farting all the way
the omni flops the same way the cooky crumbles   and   that's casualties
for jah jack   one day you're here   and   meat for the vultures

Heads and Tales

Heads   and   tales of worse were circulating   all the time
By the dollar
            and they still learn street Spanish   playing
Soccer   or   tennis   and   of course   every body
Wants to learn to dance   street Spanish   and
Love the flesh language   merengue   on hot soppy wet

Nights of manhattan summers crossing class lines   all
At least for a new York minute   that ol' who's sayin' what
To whom after that guy got a walk against a red
Tide bending in breezes sounding of the gliders versus
The drones   it felt like a park of lethalities

It was written years later   lights too bright
All pictures bad as over exposures of flesh
Opened in milliseconds   and   you said they
Were harm less when it was you   not all the hurt
And   harm no one should have to just cause

You had your flame throwers at domestic disputes
And   da shit hit de fan   and   back fired all over in
Spades   and   spics   and   you stoppin' domestic disputes
In the very sky above every body on this block
And   they had to stop running full court with no ref

In the summer time 'cause every fall cuts bad now
Wanting to know about the final cut where bandaging
Can't help an opened heart the nurses want to
Massage all night long with no treat meant planning
And   the head surgeon was stopped by the multi verse

Guards who spoke often   and   long   with no purpose
All out rages were banned   punished by exile to
The shark mills where they   required to place
Their teeth with no gloves often preceding no hands
No elbows   no arms   to the shoulder sockets   little ones lost

Being chased by showers of semantic shadows
Arrangements of sheer objects   ups   and   downs
So look the same(d)   so forget full this environment
As a whole destitute of frames   and   very incontinent
Posing as continentals in a bank   or   a map sent

By a national geographic spy waiting for you behind
Paragraphs   and   longitudes   latitudes living with
Whores of plausibilities threatening to turn them
In to princes of solitary con fine meants con fineries
Con founding fairy tales   and   angels of fine tortures

They're o' saying   not seeing   you're waiting even in the last
Of gloves when it's cold like that   it's time to play some
Thing else for a change   how a bout a chester field
You could wear   or   smoke in the bleachers with a very
Progressive mob of radical thinkers out for blood   and

Prestige   a mouth full of stage lines   or   radio   and
Comic strippers on short rest from thought missing
Signs eloquently as redd foxx after 3 boiler makers
Whose ligns of work(s) kept this going so the planes
And   boats   and   guns   and   rockets   and   h bombs

Could just grow like weeds on speed's finer gears
Creature(s) of the darks cavort in the parks every body
Was scared to enter without marine escorts   and   who
Wants to be a marine if there's a job about anything
But dodging bullets   and   missiles   and   pungi sticks   and

36

Caucasian leopards   and   tigers roaming hills in stealthy
Robes   hoping for biologists   and   ecologists   and   archaeologists
Lists of students   or   grazing to keep them all alive   and
Drive out developers with poison darts dis guised as harm
Less snakes   and   jays   and   o'jays   and   rays of smokes !!

Praxiathentics !!

Is it all be coming hideously ugly   or   just part of it
A part hidden from capes of good hopes   finally groan
And   Scandrick   these dark matters'   and   firm
You mean they didn't burn her   witch that she was
Those con junctions not to be tied

To a steak   and   fry with butter   and   garlics
Aptly for a real hot time   pulled off like toffee
On a red hot sunny after noon hopin' for an oasis   or
Trans fusion   or   can't stop for tripping on all those
Selves still In a marathon whose finish lines

Had dissipated in empty fig juice casks   on
An inter continental panel truck   with   an expert
Team of drivers swilling their own bad jokes   smokin'
A mix of crack   ketamine   thinkin' about getting' back home
After they get a final message on split dis scene   unseen   obscenics

And   obsolete as a flivver in a matted jungle patch
Pushing very slowly like bad propaganda you talk about
Your enemies with   while   some meet signing paper
Washing Benjamin again   and   over an operation so clean
People have sacrificed them selves in the way   and   slide corpuscles

In to sewage systems in search of treatments there   so
Look ma no hands for real   and   others with no feats afoot
'cause it kept dripping in so many places as could be found
In the wrong places an ace of clubs   and   mace may be leading
Them down roads

Rutted   they say it's possible to feel some thing here   but
No one said what   there's a chalupa in your futures 'cause

It's all right to break the bank with a hammer of dollars   and
An old fashioned collection of dynamite caps you screw
To the head of each department   or   else

A kind of yellow fever sluiced in to chemistry sets   and
The researchers put a halt to a current of heat running
Circles around the calculator of the moment   there
Are daily catastrophic plants wanting to happen in the city
Where they keep the water for a high rise tree

Gonna go for a long time sayin' what's there ain't
While waiting for a response tellin' what's the next step
When he said what you waitin' for   she said nuthin'
But it don't connect securely   and   we can't go on
With out things like what ain't   ya know waddah means

Well come to paradise   and   no trespassing signs in
The yard of things you stand there in wander   you
Wonder should you take a chance   and   make a jump
Or   bereft of danger a life time thru   and   didn't eliot
Say it better than marvel

Until rap brown did a royal flush answering any questions
In street poetry   but   did blacks   cops   and   shady persons
Really own that nice little bar with a great juke box   and
Well mannered brothers   and   sisters   and   it was in
That changing neighbor hood

On manhattan's so called upper west side   be low Columbia
And   west harlem which had been a changing neighbor hood
And   continues since the first modern urban war fare took place
On 84th street in '84   and   mixing had taken place as the light
Skinned Spanish speakers moved darker family in to

Apartments   and brown stones became s.r.o.s   and   since
Urban renewals turned them back in to town houses   and
Book stores couldn't make rents   and   the 'ricans   and
Cubanos get priced out   or   in to isolated/isolating projects
And   now the children go to private schools   and   learn spanish

Defense Offense Back Fence

defense   offense   back fence   and   the one around the
    gold yard
barkin' like a devil dog   keeps some on the plantation of
    things   that

don't care for you no matter how good the bass is   and
    stealin' home's
more den gospel no matter where you are this sound
    happens   don't

make no matter   other sounds loud as can be dis   rhythmic riff is
happening   and   you could still hear it when armies off others

to establish deaf zones where it was loudest   and   people(s)
were observed dancing   which   when out lawed even public fidgets

6 months   and   humming   or   whistling in public 2 years of
    hard labor
and   drummers had their hands broken as did piano players   and

music news from out side was for bidden   it was rumored
    many were
dis appeared   and   cleff   and   staff marks left on side walks   or

sand dunes hinted that some thing was wrong   but   futures like
    this were
officially denied   and   who knows   weren't there divine signs
    every night

and   horses too   like a stampede of dust   and   no sounds   if it
    wasn't here
you'd think it was weird swingin' a way   or   taking
    every thing you can   you

41

wanna get a good con duct in wars against the homies   and   roll
your owns in those alleys the lucky make time in   make love in
    and   no

bodies can hide from the truth   being on public tv provided by
    cops   who
never need to leave their station house   and   send holograms to
    courts   and

make testimonies with those hip hop stances authorities had legally
    co opted
to further blur lines   and   furrow brows   unless you were really in
    the know

about what few knew   and   were more hungry   and   stodgid (sic)
what went on be for(e) only more dogged   surprise   could get in
    the way(s)   of

these cogs   and   their mobiles   as impossible as this thing you
    say   you
want free dom   justice   and   equality   in this process   you're so
    fast   you

can't participate except in vague dusky hotels   in obscure   obsolete
    cities   where
the help seemed to say none here   jack   and   negotiators had just
    started   with

out you again easily since they lived there   and   you had trouble
    getting in
the door till the boss sent a picture of you   and   a quick finger
    prick   check

your dna be in the right places   as   one of your teams is
    winning   and   other
losing every bag out of tricks   the trick of bags got you   and
    there's alotta

alligators who can't see in the dark and   bump in to you   if   you
    don't pay
attention to rules from a bag   dad   trickle trickle about the jewels
    in that

ring of fire   gold running down your leg   in the book where it
    was some
body's gold getting beau coup attention in the fillipines where
    this was

goin" on at   planting an other preposition at the end of a
    sentence   tho'
you can be tricked   'cause   it didn't stop there   a relic aspiced
    in deep

acting   thirsting   still nothing but all brazen bad   not adrift but
    no go here

don't care for soul   no matter how good the bass is   and   stealin'
    homes'
more den gospel   no matter   where you are this sound happen's

This We Lived to See

this we lived to see all so
that   which was very hip

in the cities by the late 50s
had taken over   but   at least

50 years too late logo real diarrhea
fever dreamer our man snake   said

have no fear   every thing is cool   the coast
is clear   and   clean   and   the tide's out

way out there   new wave   new jazz   and
recording equipment devices   and   hearts alive

with dis beat   and   dat beat   so look up me hearties
red glow may be new sun   and   not what you think   unless

it starts approaching   and   you know nothing can be done   and
neither you   and   goin' home exist now   so still around

later on   there's so many stars painted on that ceiling   of
things   how they got wired to blinkin'   and   thinking

is a mystery   which   may be an opera some day   all
ways in the movies   movies in you too   some day(s)

you'll wish you was a star   written on the side(s)   of
your head in red as can be   you're now a banner   being

waved by too many at once how can a camera catch you
and   only you   for the folks back home to remember   red

who you probably were at that last revolutionary moment
manning the barricade(s)   gloriously bloody   no oscars

just buzzards   and   lotsa what the fucks   propping each other
up   waiting for the next film makers   who   were waiting on

their patrons   who   were waiting for their coupons   which
some one was taking from the mail box in the greater cloud

back to the relief pitchers
and   pictures of relief   pitchers of relief spilt on the market   as

perpetrators were allowed to replace use less law enforce meant
agencies   and   on   to those imaginary and sniping at you

whisps in the air   of   just a thought   of   a put down
you swoop in

they think you a rock star on a run   from   debilitating   inspirational
riches to rags 'cause all your friends were shooting up too   and

it felt good in this guise   you conquered never going to wars   and
killing tunes in the hearts of the devils' army so busy sniping   at

your repertoire of foggy personae   in some chapters you take gold
to your wife   and   family   from the villainous   and treacherous

business of pushing truth mobiles to hang from lamp posts   glowing
at mid night   the pictures   of   enemies   of all the people you like   and

the message is arm your selves   or   harm your selves   and   the sound
is   of course   part   of   the picture you want to scream so hard in   so

you break the screen to shreds   and   demand a refund   of course
there's these devils beyond the screen too   just like you   except

there's gettin' to be so many colors people don't know what to do
more   and   more often   and   a monster of a system lurking

sooner   looking closer than we admit to

The Mad Men of Clutches

the mad men of clutches
on front street flexing

methodistas
on the cause way it was juiced   and
pusillanimous when they let one out there   and
swear it was accidental   tell you it was really bad then

and   now such a blood bath you get used to
it stalin said a statistic   or   was it kissinger
just enough for a pipe full perfesser so high

droppin' exploits   and   expletives mit dat accent
who's got the real stuff around here   before

they close the gates   and   dogs go on sentry
so much is happening   a nasty wicked curve ball
would be the strength test
offices of rate makers   and   state breakers

before
the vote goes down the river
the street gangs settled in licking wounds   and

snorting pipe dreams post season paranoias crawling
around the fields receptors like bugs in the grasses

stealing signs hoping for more strike outs   before
those crushing touch downs   and   swat teams

ready to go to the rim(s) with out final orders
while a nurses' school had developed a new curriculum   for

taking temperatures   and   giving trans fusions   while
tricks were turned splendidly on market corners   where

bookies in brooks bros finery moved bucks   fingered finks
there was the muscular deaf mute and
me all most froze on the way back from spring field   as
it turned winter grey dusks shared   sleet be coming snow

the only white kid who'd play
with an us for a while   the grimace   the uunnnnnhhh !! sound

riffling the air   an us wondering how far it would go   if
he ever hit the ball good in the field   and   could really throw   and

later   then we began to work   only one hen left   hence   few to none
eggs   and   she may be hiding them from an us   if

still layin'   strange sentiment for us
as fellow creatures

we would still love to eat fresh egg(s) in the morning
without leaving the house   and   spending money

every   and   each moment a proto type of the next
for it too   yet   being included losing in dust swirls

of   seconds   and   referees to keep the banks opening
on time   and   more clerks making more time with more

secretaries on more desks than any time in measured civilization

crews have a gossip column
robots will soon deactivate
its scandalous assertions
such is life

the missing of bodies and souls friends and lovers

the missing of bodies and souls friends and lovers
in places no longer there except when it counts   for

some thing so special you can actually feel it   you
can   you all   after can   you can feel it   and   it was good   that

you could feel it all   after all   and   may be you are the ghost
and   haven't seen it yet 'cause you ain't carryin' no crosses   or

crossed swords
on that spot once wilderness   was thing sweating   to

the max   and   you got no sense of smell around you   but
know a rose from a giant corn stalk   you like to drink gin and
      tonic   now

toucha bitters lime beef eaters you know   and   pork   and   chicken
and   every meat you can name before catchin' fish too   a starter

relieves a center   shoots threes   holds   and   rebounds   while
lions slouch towards a white line in all of the countries   with

no return clauses signed by their agents   and   witnessed   by
jailers   and   delilahs   with cosmetic resumes ringing falsely   and

in so many play grounds across the land no longer did the pusher
man have to work except to advertise 'cause even the cops were selling

good shit   so   why not   and   it seemed like a good idea at the time
every body gets some   you dig   but   one thing about cops is

they got guns   and   guess who ain't like every body else

when you cover your ass you gotta watch your back too . no
	scratchin' only
sharp things and dossiers and financial ruins a maniac of

loghorreatics thrown out of a door of dictionaries pleading for
	relevant lines
in hagiographies of sounds more miraculous than the first
	abracadabras and

genies hiding out in bottles of thunder bird and black velvets in
	crocks of
pitter patterns on a fling singing their gizzards off and on the shelf

dabbles of trickle down drowning thousands in patrician mirth born
target practice rising through ruckus pursuing king of the mountain

ship and titles not invented still worthy and shapely ho !!
talked about a shoot out with jw dant it was a hundred proof but

they were two fisted well armed will full and no good sense at
	all with
a metabolism in a few centuries for ward would power rockets but

pin all the crimes in the world you can find and you found more
than you

had numbers for and you were the last on your block to find this out
it's suburban on the rocks exurbs a literary fancy gated is in
the poor is out

ya know at one time there were credentialed people
who couldn't curve an illusion fed to the masses in

spite of eyes with and with out bifocals big screens on the

   road(s) of
things to mandalay or zanzibar the bus to hackensack commuter
so many escapes from the world's at war on your door step and

there's no side you're on but the target practice again you bet again
the bulls'eyes jump suits in orange and a glow red heart front
   and back
you wanted to score baskets got balooned on the way

shrinking a way from what's

shrinking a way from what's got you in sides   and
you get to pay them 'cause good credit's part of your

mental health   and   what's really eating at you is buried   in
these efforts at sweeping wolves away from the door jams   and
the other doo whoppers hangin' at your crib

recording studios are searchin' for it still

a dance beats a war

by all means   and   let's try on another one of these reality buttons
considered a privelege out side wheel(s) of karma if you believe
    of course

'cause asteroids don't die like astro nauts   and   land differently
    so far
so good   over there hum drumming aging dumbing   and
    all there is

to see is the same blocks to walk dogs around   and   around   and
then   feed them a mix   that long word was a centipede cesaire said

and   wine could be dropped   but didn't   after an other homer   fine
name for what's taken home   with   a story where you can buy pizza

among the poets ready to sprinkle in your ears   and   no napkins
as fingers dirty with all kinds of phrases   nasty claws   blood

dripping through the pages   you   wanting a trans fusion   and
a scotch on the rock piles of thesaurus surrounded by snakes

with gumptious land shades of heather   and   diamond   and
coral fixed with silver   you wanted turquoise on the palette

there's a library of things you're no longer able to do   and   no
copy rights exist there so you better get going   while   you can

still read   and   follow good sense on the page   and   chase
a way the flies at the same time   shoe fly   shoe

there were no score keepers till the hospital closed
white powders on the run   on the mirror   on
the pharmacy palette   or   a revolutionary mind thinkin'

a border's gonna close on either them   or   us   and   logistics
is more hit   and   run   than logicus II the one they nick named

out of sight behind shades   talkin hipoisie   and   mucho shit
your mind a mush mobile   and   all that jassed up action in
a corner talkathon   and   amounted to the what

I am the mission exiled to the burbovilles

I am the mission exiled to the burbovilles
Where there are many cons
leave you wondering
Oh shit !! will it happen here
why not this hard road

You can't park here 'cause it might happen here
The mothers of invention   50 years-a-go   said it is

And   lots believe still   zapped   or   not   missing visions
Of that suzy cream cheese effect   shooting up in

The valley   and   the alley
Even under the nipple   spots near elbows
Thrown   and   fumbles in the red zone

it's just a game to keep
Working accountants off the side lines   and

In their cells where slyly   and   shyly they rule
rewarded with raises more often than the
Politicians voting them selves a bit   this is how

Life can bore   unable to excite motility bugs
No anxiety on the surfaces
you think old school stuff   like holding
Action(s) no body can see   and   that's why they get paid

The world of boring   every day   we here don't get thermo nuclearized
Like an old Philip wylie might hint at   and   how many cold wars
Does it take to make the kind of miss take can't be taken back
And   a genuine kabloowee happens all over the place
And   they said the sub way's safe now   take the a trane home !!

And   still could only say no   silently to those great powers
And   still so much loneliness   was it the bull's eye   or   the bull shit
Garnering votes on the corner   in one corner   and   sheer murder
In the other   and   they swore it was gonna be a fair one   like
They used to have in monogamy

On a stage   hiding love in steps
That's how civilization spreads
with no wholes
Barred   or guarded by the church   master with his hold
On gods   and   what ever   a champ of things

It's a winner we want   time after time   after
What act(s) of rebellion count now   and   how do we know
Where on that cosmic calculus of acts with meanings
we knew on the street
That clock timing in breath   and   blood pulsing   and
Veining around the hood

You Must Remember This

In vincible   and   in trepid like god used to be
You must remember this   the pyramids built
Them selves by mass hypnosis we're part of now
Is when stones   and   minds were a hive   is what
They thought   there   on their haunches   looking up

Wards   where the infidels still managed to eke out
Their own magics   but   were unable to reproduce
Them   or   their selves   and   centuries of war fares
Now existed only on the earth   they said if it weren't
For them blue gooders   and   the instruments they got

And   there is a some one contemplating   this
Whole trip   and   what it is   feelings have no names
Until the eco system induces word   wall   witches
Made for the worlds   there   hoping   how more
People(s) making more music(s) might induce

More celestial routes to more pacem in terris
Even from a dead pope who couldn't project
Mind   thought if there were time to do it   'cause
So much hurry in war world(s)   and   who's got the
Time to look up and may be die 'cause there

Was the target   and   often the sound of a buzzing
Bomb can be thought projected   too   so who knows
What can be con fusing   and   may be you feel drums
Sensations before you notice   you're steppin' it
A bit different   and   you begin to listen for some thing

Else   and   you catch some things in the ear   the vibes
You been steppin' to   all most a melody   differentiating

Its selves   bits of it's a some place else song some
Bodies are makin' in this shit   when you could just
Some how(s) change your channels   so to speak   then stop

No more petty minded massacres as you think of a way
Out   out no more   let's see what happens when we make
More of these   ad infinitum   beyond human ideas about the
Experiencing of it   they call astro physics   or   plain ol' physics
Too   tho' good measure(s) meant were made   and   placed

Creaturely poly maths   it wasn't just bad poetry in the
Closets of time   but   whole constellations could be on a
Hit list   verified by all the earthly intelligence agencies
That could be bought   or   by black mails brought nailed
To beds of grass   and   the insects saved from the

Germicides for tortures   post modern tapestries at show
And   tell degrees In   and   of atrocities at their very best(s)
Travesties   think in pacem in terris all the time   wine   or
Not of the swine   but   what's not in some places burning
With gotta such a magnificent stand   may be stance

Forgotten being   being forgotten   others'   not so   at first
Then a rush of paranoias   this is all invented of course
But   the nervous system doesn't lie like a mind awry can
Lil' boy was all ways stuck in this shit no matter his   and
Her ages   all ways each   all   every   both   all   every

That   mantra'd all over   both   all   every   ways to escape
Gifted   divine   like it or not   all efforts futile   kickin' in
To every lack   caught 'em again   caught over   and   over
And   stuffed with all kindsa needs you know about
A quaw drafta   hoping   engaging non sense   et   cetering(s)

As if healing were still possible   prime time ass whole(s)
Pacem in terris   pacem   pacem   pacem to what avail in
Terris   pacem   pacem in terris over   and over   implored of this
Duration   vacancy   vacant sea   vacant si   see   nothing   si   si
'cause every body's got its own bad days   and   nights   too   !!!!!!!!!!!!!!

About the editors and the back ground of the book (From We Came To Play: Writings on Basketball)

I

in harlem on my mind   there's a picture
of my daddy van der zee's magic camera made
seated on the steps of the alpha phi alpha house
with his team mates gathered about the game of basket ball
in the negro in sports there's a picture
of my grand father   my momma's daddy   standing
amongst his team mates
                                   washington ymca national champs '09-'10
in the room of disappointments where my heart is
constant replaying of me failing at basket ball
on every court   in doors and out I ran on
                                                          and that's a
whole lot
stirs me to filch out stills of
how the failure begain in bed stuy
continued through new england harlem and north philly
then returned to the magic island of Manhattan
where the eighty seventh street old man's basket ball association
held court for almost a year
                                   we gloriously shoveled snow to
                                                                         in '68

II

Stills flicking and flickering in
to one
            an other
                                   cavalcading images
be hind the back

be tween the legs

then flight

lost ins i'm fixed at viewing

collagings

all labors of all loves
of this more than game
o' i swear

more than

there's lennie wilkens getting his chops together
in the low ceilinged court of holy rosary with alton walden
and tommy watkins jr   Lennie was an altar boy there too

there's lennie at the garden
in the finals of the nit my father took me to
leading providence to a championship

determined left handed
dribble then the little pop shot
again and again

that's lennie in the midst of the boys' high ethos
from which young men brought skills and pride
to many peoples all over this land

finally   the world

si hugo green
solly walker
al barden
billy burwell
eddie simmons
john lagoff
jackie Jackson
tommie davis
connie hawkins
vaughn harper
there there were the guys from lane

                                        art howard
                                    the daniels brothers
                                        jake Jordan
                                    richie chink gaines

III

You can sight these things in the '50s
where ten st sends a 5 to the pros but don't get invited no wheres
            barnett   barnhill   finley   warley   et al
where sherman white and leroy smith don't get a chance to transform
            the game with our new thing and we must wait for elgin and
                    oscar
where the sense of eliteness and egalitarianism entwined often elicited
    an ambience of the polis as popular and positive
                                        more seemed possible
where but on these basketball courts

in this space I virtually reek of
films   stories   poems   novels

                            calling for vernacular artists
                            to even take this now cyberspace
                            so that the fall out of history
                            descends in the true full colors
                            it arose from
                                        pre green powers
when i'd return from boarding school
where i'd shoot baskets on saturday nights
                                    often alone
rather than attend the movies all students saw
billy pickens made sure i got to see the hot teams

when my family moved to harlem
john and ed Norton

                    the whole eddie's cabal
turned me on to the battle ground
                                        the rucker's tournament

i can remember a little court in the school yard of ps 43
where al lynch and eugene pilgrim and eddie simmons would
to no avail try to help me improve my game
                                        my spirit was all
                                        ways better than my skills

one year I saw clinton upset boys' at the city champs
in the same trounament the next year i saw head to head
connie hawkins and roger brown
                        roger was seventeen for 34. total of 39
                            no tellin how many would be 3s now
                        but boys' wouldn't blow the finals again
                            and the hawk really did fly then

IV

there's a slow mo of me scoring
fewer and fewer in California
where i sight the knicks finaly   winning
                            after all the times
                            me and pop had been to the garden
                            and they'd lost
                                                    since '49
on a tv in a motel room in redding
with a lovely woman who'd more than befriended me
                                        in spite of my selves
and the director of the local poverty program
i'd gone up there to do a job for
                        clyde   skull   dollar bill
                        topping the wilt and jerry show

she and I were still companions where
i literally bumped in john ross who
picked up the ball i'd fumbled away
in the editing of this book

                                    he scored any way

as i scrambled to group therapy
one saturday morning in seventy one
from her apartment on romolo place in north beach

john and i hadn't seen each other since '58
when he left greenwhich village for Chiapas
        his book documenting the organized struggle of
        native american peoples against entrenched forces of greed there
        won an american book award last year from
        the before columbus foundation

                                    rebellion from the roots
                                    common courage press

and he and i had met in sag harbor long island
due to friends family and fortuity of bad weather
which drove his camping family to seek shelter
at least on the porch of a running buddy's folks' summer home

  this was the summer of '50   or was it '51 john

                                            now in mexico

the start of a long friend ship

it turns out that his mother and my aunt had collaborated
occasionally doing theatrical publicity in the big apple
that was during the 2nd world war his step father
who left the war from the merchant marines and
did stints with the sf art institute and a globe trotter b team
before his career on canvass as an abstract expressionist
had placed a basket with a net in the grand loft

they lived in on west broad way

no stock brokers there then

it was a place visions grew from
a place and play ground all in one
to us raised in the brown stone tradition
we sub wayed there   and in a few years
the loft became a salon and party pad

the cops came more than once
up six flights

no elevator

where hungry and high spirits found
miles and camus and Ellison and yoga
and chicago green and oscar and elgin
mixed with monk and la playa's coco secos
talking and dancing till the night time
slipped into the right time before coming of light

some of these brothers and sisters
we did significant growing up with
john and i are still in touch with
as well as a whiff of turpentine and oil paint
and sun beams within the net
under the sky light

V

John couldn't play basket ball any better than me
but that didn't stop him either and he says a certain group
of non spanish speaking hoopsters on the dusty court in Chiapas
have nick named him el swish

now there's a story

since the seventies though
each of us has done more watching

and talking about basket ball than playing
david henderson's one of the persons I talked to
he'd been one of us psychedelic swashbucklers
running full court ball on eighty seventh street
much nearer to columbus ave than central park west
we ran on a shortened court but we rand and ran
and there too was salon and party the women
indulging our sweat and funk to sly and 'trane
as we comingled round ball with liberation talk
and poetry and painting in a neighborhood where
one side of the court was gentrified brown stones
and the other rail road tenements which
a neighborhood group led by an ex national guardian writer turned
          organizer
would ultimately liberate from a housing authority
with little concern for poor people with large families
I brought the drama of this court
to the work I did with john o'neal
and a team of writers and performers
who made "aint no use in goin' home"
and it crucially informed one of the scenes
when it was produced at alice arts in Oakland
in the late '80s
                    john o in the role of junebug jabbo jones
is it coincidence or synchronicity
john ross and david Henderson are
friends of mine   each of whose poetry
has influenced me and my writing over the years
about a basketball book or project or
                              who knows
                                  what aobut johnnie ace
so that when richard grossinger
got in touch with me   it was about
this book through David who'd remembered
and passed it on

VI

at the time of this writing i work
as a community mental health counselor
in the mission district of san Francisco
where i've lived for many years now though
all of my family's in the north east and
my father who also played for the harlem ymca
died on cape cod where he'd retired with his beloved blossom

john ross is living and writing in mexico city
and his family in the north east too
his son dante is a knick fanatic
and a producer of rap

the confluence of spirit and matter
involving persons touched by round ball
surprise me still

      in a sport column here several years ago
      kc jones cited mr sadalla a math and gym teacher
      at a jhs here who'd encouraged him   and gail sadalla
      and his daughter helped keep the spirits of john and i
      together
      so each of us were trying to write and be active
      in spite of our selves
                   and because
                          just because
      at a cal poets in the schools' benefit

the grand son of one of my father's team mates is a performer too
and his partner in performance was the son of a painter
a running buddy of john wideman at u of p

out of this stuff comes my participation
in this book my father and his friends
hipped me to years before my eyes began to recognize possibilities

this book that wouldn't exist without the work of jr
            or the conversations with David

                              or the phone calls
                              and persistence of Richard

enjoy
            qr hand jr

Originally published in the 1968 classic, *Black Fire*, an anthology of African American writing, edited by Amiri Baraka (Leroi Jones) and Larry Neal, which has recently been reproduced by Black Classics Press, **Q. R. Hand, Jr.** is the author of three poetry books, *i speak to the poet in man* (jukebox press), *how sweet it is* (Zeitgeist Press), and *whose really blues, new & selected poems* (Taurean Horn Press). He is an original member of the Wordwind Chorus, a Bay Area quartet that has performed poetry with jazz for over twenty years. Wordwind has one cd, *we are of the saying*. He was the 2012 Recipient of the Pen Oakland REGINALD LOCKETT LIFETIME ACHIEVEMENT AWARD.

"There's a ship
The Black Freighter
With a skull on it's masthead
Will be coming in"

— Nina Simone, Pirate Jenny

Black Freighter Press publishes revolutionary books. committed to the exploration of liberation, using art to transform consciousness. A platform for Black and Brown writers to honor ancestry and propel radical imagination.